Colors in Nature

Orange

by Martha E. H. Rustad

Bullfrog
Books

Ideas for Parents and Teachers

Bullfrog Books let children practice reading informational text at the earliest reading levels. Repetition, familiar words, and photo labels support early readers.

Before Reading

- Discuss the cover photo. What does it tell them?
- Look at the picture glossary together. Read and discuss the words.

Read the Book

- "Walk" through the book and look at the photos. Let the child ask questions. Point out the photo labels.
- Read the book to the child, or have him or her read independently.

After Reading

- Prompt the child to think more. Ask: What orange things do you see outside? Are they natural or man-made?

For Markus, as orange was once your second-favorite color.
—MEHR

Bullfrog Books are published by Jump!
5357 Penn Avenue South
Minneapolis, MN 55419
www.jumplibrary.com

Library of Congress Cataloging-in-Publication Data
Rustad, Martha E. H. (Martha Elizabeth Hillman), 1975-
 Orange / By Martha E. H. Rustad.
    pages cm. -- (Colors in nature)
 Includes bibliographical references and index.
 Summary: "This photo-illustrated book for early readers tells about plants, animals, and how orange works in the natural world. Includes picture glossary"--Provided by publisher.
  ISBN-13: 978-1-62031-037-3 (hardcover) ISBN-13: 978-1-62496-038-3 (ebook)
 1. Color in nature--Juvenile literature. 2. Orange--Juvenile literature. I. Title.
 QC495.5.R88 2014
 535.6--dc23   2012039681

Series Editor   Rebecca Glaser
Book Designer   Ellen Huber
Photo Researcher   Heather Dreisbach

Photo Credits: Alamy, 23tl; Corbis, 20–21, 23tr; Dreamstime, 3; Getty Images, 11, 13; Shutterstock, cover, 1, 4, 5, 6–7, 8–9, 10, 12, 15, 16, 22a, 22b, 22c, 22d, 23bl, 23mr, 24; Superstock, 14, 17, 18–19, 23ml, 23b

Printed in the United States of America at Corporate Graphics, North Mankato, Minnesota.
4-2013 / PO 1003

10 9 8 7 6 5 4 3 2 1

Table of Contents

Looking for Orange

Where do you see orange?
Look around in nature.

I see a monarch butterfly.

Why is it orange?

Orange warns birds that it tastes bad.

I see a sunset.
Why is the sky orange?

Dust makes it look orange.

I see an orange.
Why is it orange?

It changes color
when it is ripe.

I see a pumpkin. Why is it orange?

It is ready to be picked.

I see a tiger.

Why does it have
orange stripes?

Stripes hide it
in tall grasses.

I see a lily.
Why is it orange?

Bright colors
help bees find it.

17

I see a clownfish.

Why is it orange?

The color tells other fish not to eat it.

I see an octopus.

Why is it orange?

It changes
color to hide.

Where do you
see orange?

21

Shades of Orange

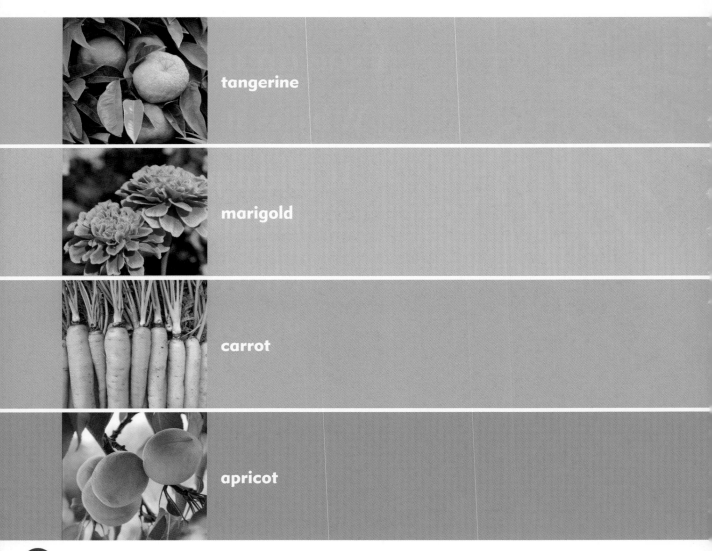

tangerine

marigold

carrot

apricot

Photo Glossary

butterfly
An insect with four colorful wings.

octopus
An ocean animal with eight tentacles.

clownfish
A small ocean fish with stripes.

sunset
Colors and light seen in the sky as the sun goes down.

lily
A plant that grows from a bulb and has a flower shaped like a trumpet.

tiger
A large striped cat that lives in forests in Asia.

Index

To Learn More

Learning more is as easy as 1, 2, 3.

1) Go to www.factsurfer.com

2) Enter "orange" into the search box.

3) Click the "Surf" button to see a list of websites.

With factsurfer.com, finding more information is just a click away.